EMPOWER YOUR MONEY

101 Simple Ways for Female Entrepreneurs to Create Financial Freedom

ANGELA DUNCAN

Founder, EmpowerHERMoney

DEDICATION

To my dearest daughter Isela,

For your unwavering love, endless inspiration, and the boundless joys you bring to my life.

You are the light that guides my words, and this book is a testament to that love and wisdom you have imparted to me.

With all my love,

Angela Duncan

WHAT OTHERS ARE SAYING ABOUT ANGELA DUNCAN

"If you're looking for a financial coach, you've found her. Working with Angela has been completely life changing. Not only is she extremely professional and knows her stuff, she's going to take the time to get to know you, understand your needs, and how to execute to the next level."
- **Rebecca Tisbe**, CEO of JVR Freight LLC

"Angela is a true professional. She not only cares for her clients she goes well beyond the call of duty. I would highly recommend her!"
- **Jennifer Martinez**, VP of Mortgage Lending, CrossCountry Mortgage

"Angela Duncan is the force to install hope in those who are lost, who need guidance with financing and will be inspired by her story of how she continues to be the beacon of hope for many. I highly recommend working with Angela as she is already impacting many lives, including mine."
- **Jeff J. Cunningham**, CEO of Changing Lives Consulting

MOTIVATE AND INSPIRE OTHERS!

"Share This Book"

Retail $19.95

Special Quantity Discounts

5-20 Books	$17.95
21-99 Books	$15.95
100-499 Books	$13.95
500-999 Books	$11.95
1,000+ Books	$10.95

To Place an Order Contact:

info@EmpowerHERmoney.com
(305) 876-6050

THE IDEAL PROFESSIONAL SPEAKER FOR YOUR NEXT EVENT!

Any organization that wants to develop their people to become "extraordinary," needs to hire Angela for a keynote and/or workshop training!

To Contact Or Book Angela To Speak:

info@EmpowerHERmoney.com
www.EmpowerHERmoney.com

THE IDEAL COACH FOR YOU!

If you're ready to overcome financial
challenges, have major breakthroughs and
achieve your financial goals and dreams,
then you will love having Angela Duncan as
your coach!

CONTACT ANGELA NOW!

www.EmpowerHERmoney.om
(305) 876-6050
info@EmpowerHERmoney.com

Best return on investment is to

invest in yourself first—

podcasts,
books,
webinars,
coaching programs
are a great start!

You are
one connection,
one idea, and one
implementation
away from

achieving your

financial goals

Contribute to your retirement account before any children's college education plan. They can get a loan for college,

you cannot get a loan for retirement.

Get OUT of credit card debt

BEFORE you start investing!

Research index funds or ETF's as a **COST EFFECTIVE** way to participate in the stock market!

Change out your closet by hosting a clothing swap.

Invite friends over with their new or gently used clothing and swap items.

Other swap party ideas for **kid's toys, alcohol, books, make-up, or jewelry.**

Host a themed potluck at your home, switch homes with your friends.

Bring Tupperware for left-overs.

Host a game night

instead of going to see a new show or event.

After Christmas, **host a re-gift party** to get rid of those unwanted gifts for something you may use.

If you are a business owner and use your home to host meetings,

learn the Augusta Rule.

Carry small amounts of cash to avoid high out-of-network ATM fee's.

You can attend college for free.

Several colleges in the U.S. offer free tuition not based on financial need. Do your research!

If you are renting,

you <u>NEED</u> renters' insurance.

Many credit card companies **waive the annual fee for active military members.** Thank you for your service.

When you travel, ask the **hotel concierge** for their **best money saving tips.**

Shop around
for insurance
at every
renewal date
**AND compare
COVERAGES,
not just
the rate.**

If you have children, look at term life insurance. And if you are married with children, **get life insurance on BOTH husband and wife.**

NEGOTIATE

your cable, internet, or phone bills.

Have money sitting in a savings account? Shop around for the **highest paying interest rate in an FDIC bank.**

Wash your clothes in cold water.

It saves money on your electric bill and your color will last longer.

Get an **accountability coach** to hold you *accountable* on your **financial goals.**

When selling your used items online, **research fees** each app charges to get the most money for your sold items.

When purchasing larger items, **set a time limit you must wait** to shop around before making those larger purchases.

4 Biggest

RISKS

that will affect your
retirement:

Market returns,
cost of health care,
inflation, and out
living your money.

If your employer offers a match for your 401k or employer sponsored retirement program, **take FULL ADVANTAGE OF THE MATCH before contributing to an outside retirement account.**

If you are relatively healthy, **consider a higher deductible** health insurance plan **and an HSA account.**

*Have an extra room
in your home?*

Consider AIRBNB or renting to traveling nurses.

You are not too young to have a will or estate plan.

If you are over 18, create one with a professional today.

Review your
credit card
statements
every month
for unauthorized
charges.

Review your
credit report
ANNUALLY
for mistakes!

Check

www. unclaimed.org

The National Association of Unclaimed property –

you may be owed money from a utility deposit or account you forgot about!

Increasing your credit limit on your credit card may boost your credit score. **Be careful not to get further into debt with this TIP.**

Prioritize paying down credit cards by interest

rates, higher the rate, tackle that debt first.

Consider a **1031 Exchange when you sell a rental property** to defer taxes.

Look for free apps that pay you to take a survey. **SURVEYS ON THE GO** is a great one to try.

Planning to go on vacation?

Consider swapping houses,

allow someone to stay at your home while having a benefit to use another person's home.

Inexpensive way to vacation is to

RENT an RV.

Several app's available for this driving vacation.

No longer using that bicycle? Yep, there is an app to rent that out too!

Have spare tools in your garage? Several app's available to help you **get paid to loan out your tools** just sitting in your garage.

Live in a unique home? Consider renting your home out to Hollywood for movies or shows being filmed in your area.

Pick
2 days
every week
as your
"no spend"
days.

Pack your work lunch.

Lose weight.

Save money.

Eat healthier.

Enjoy baking?
Sell gift baskets with your goodies during the holidays.

Some generic foods are made in the same factories as your brand name items.

And they usually cost 20-25% less!

Are you great at math? Consider tutoring for a **side hustle to make extra income.**

SELL THOSE AMAZING PHOTOGRAPHS you took with that high end camera.

Several apps allow you to

buy or sell gift cards.

A **secured credit card** is a great way to **start building your credit!**

Turn your crafts
into
profit
via Etsy!

Know your numbers- income, expenses, net worth.

It's your starting point when setting money goals!

Creating a **budget to manage your money goals** is a powerful and easy to follow tool.

Shoes you wear are not an investment.

They go down in value.

Diamonds are a better investment!

No more than 30% of your take home pay

should go to rent or your mortgage payment.

Swap babysitting

with other couple friends for FREE for date nights.

AVOID

adjustable-rate mortgages or ARM's for your primary home loan.

Look for loans with no pre-payment penalties!

If rates go down,

consider refinancing your mortgage or consolidating debt.

Before buying a car, consider its twin.

A twin is a very similar car brand that sells for less.

Create a unique local experience for travelers and promote to travel agents.

There are apps that will pay you to go look at stuff, verify information and report back.

If needles do not bother you, **CONSIDER DONATING PLASMA.**

Participate in a clinical trial **for additional income.**

Look for banks that offer a sign-up bonus.

REPEAT.

Get paid to narrate audio books.

Put your chef skills to use and **offer to be an in-house party chef for events.**

Abandoned storage units go up for auction.

Bid and sell items from your unit.

Be careful not to overbid, set a limit and stick to it.

Background actors or "movie extras"

pay very little but they also provide food and *being on set is a cool experience.*

Checkout Craigslist or other sites for stores closing that have inventory.

Watch a YouTube videos on how to best sell products for profit.

SAFEGUARD
against identity theft and fraud
by choosing difficult passwords and not using the same for all your accounts.

Swap out giving your kids an allowance and

pay them for chores!

Business owners hire a financial Coach for your employees.

Every year create a visual financial goal board

with short-, mid-, and long-term financial goals.

Keep it visual!

Can't afford a gym?

Work out with household items like canned goods, brooms, water jugs.

Save money on your electric bill
by having dinner via candlelight.

Maximize your tax benefits

by hiring a professional

Have a good-sized back yard? **Grow produce and sell it at the local farmer's market.**

Buy inexpensive pots and plant seeds. Go to your local farmers market and **sell the plants once they have sprouted.**

Love shoes? Start an Instagram page and **become a brand ambassador and join** affiliate **programs.** Get paid to post about shoes.

Become a professional line waiter–

stand in line for those who hate waiting and get paid for it.

#blackfriday

Use the library
to keep reading
those new novels
or diet books,
it's free. Start
a book club.

Sign up for loyalty programs

at your favorite stores and look for free items on your birthday.

Free trial offers can be great as long as you **remember to cancel before the trial period is over!**

Watch YouTube for videos on DIY—

like laundry detergent or cleaning supplies.

DIY can also be great for holiday gifts—

both thoughtful and less expensive.

Start a savings challenge with a co-worker, set a goal, see who can reach it first. Prize is bragging rights or your child's old sports trophy you pass around the office.

Small
consistent spending habit
changes result in long
term changes
and **achieving**
your goals.

Just because
something is on sale,
doesn't mean you
buy something
you NEVER
intended to buy.

Find cheaper hobbies until you have the money to afford more expensive hobbies.

Encourage entrepreneurship to your kid's, have them start a store, a lawn mowing business, babysitting or making their own holiday gifts.

These 10 are financial advice Tips to **NEVER** follow:

Google financial tips because the internet is always right.

Quit your job and become a gamer.

Spend your
Saturdays
at Costco
as a cheap
way to **feed
your family
through free
samples.**

Sign up for every credit card possible, the more credit the better.

Start a business by **selling bottled air** in used water bottles you found in the trash.

Increase your chances of winning **scratch off tickets** by shopping at every local gas station $1 at a time.

Sell timeshares on the moon- "Lunar Vacation" is the next hot vacation trip.

Start a business by going to the dog park, listening to dog names, then **selling pet rocks.**

Take financial advice from your friend who filed for bankruptcy.

Recycle your used empty wine bottles and turn them into housewarming gifts for your friends who do not drink.

Just add a bow!

101 AND FINAL TIP:

Hire a professional to help you with your financial goals and mindset. A coach will help **keep you accountable, on track, and cheer you on** and celebrate as you reach your goals.

ONE LAST MESSAGE

Congratulations
for making it to the end of this book!

ABOUT ANGELA

Meet Angela, a woman who defied the odds and survived a childhood of abuse and poverty.

Angela Duncan was raised in Section 8 housing, welfare and working at a young age. Her journey has been marked by resilience and determination. With 25 + years of personal finance study, Angela has honed her expertise to inspire HOPE through financial literacy. Graduating with a Finance Degree from California State University San Marcos, she embarked on a diverse career in banking, financial advising, owning a top 20 RE/MAX office for 5 straight years with over $2 Billion in sales, and establishing and selling an insurance agency. Serial entrepreneur at heart.

Now, Angela is committed to closing the poverty gap by empowering others to change their financial future. She firmly believes, no matter where one starts in life, they have the power to shape their own destiny.

www.EmpowerHERmoney.com

www.FreeMoneyTipsforWomen.com

ADDITIONAL RESOURCES

Empower HER Money Presents:
Dominate YOUR Business Workshops

Work on **YOUR** Business and
Leave with **YOUR** Complete Business Plan

To Sign up for the next workshop:

www.EmpowerHERmoney.com